CONTENTS

CONTENTS

CREDITS

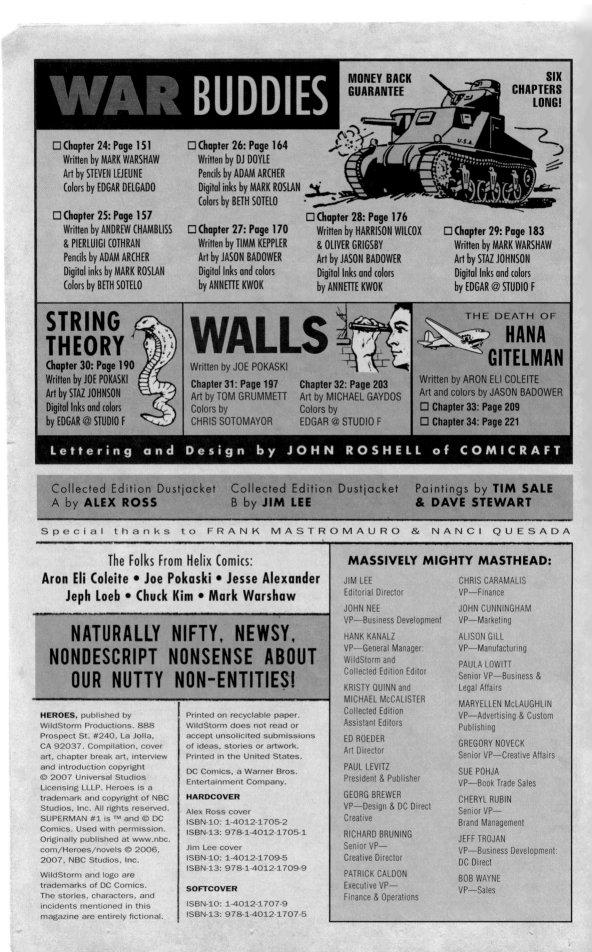

WAR BUDDIES

MONEY BACK GUARANTEE

SIX CHAPTERS LONG!

Tr

Lettering and Design by JOHN ROSHELL of COMICRAFT

Collected Edition Dustjacket A by **ALEX ROSS**

Collected Edition Dustjacket B by **JIM LEE**

Paintings by **TIM SALE & DAVE STEWART**

Special thanks to FRANK MASTROMAURO & NANCI QUESADA

The Folks From Helix Comics:
Aron Eli Coleite • Joe Pokaski • Jesse Alexander
Jeph Loeb • Chuck Kim • Mark Warshaw

NATURALLY NIFTY, NEWSY, NONDESCRIPT NONSENSE ABOUT OUR NUTTY NON-ENTITIES!

MASSIVELY MIGHTY MASTHEAD:

JIM LEE
Editorial Director

JOHN NEE
VP—Business Development

HANK KANALZ
VP—General Manager:
WildStorm and
Collected Edition Editor

KRISTY QUINN and
MICHAEL McCALISTER
Collected Edition
Assistant Editors

ED ROEDER
Art Director

PAUL LEVITZ
President & Publisher

GEORG BREWER
VP—Design & DC Direct
Creative

RICHARD BRUNING
Senior VP—
Creative Director

PATRICK CALDON
Executive VP—
Finance & Operations

CHRIS CARAMALIS
VP—Finance

JOHN CUNNINGHAM
VP—Marketing

ALISON GILL
VP—Manufacturing

PAULA LOWITT
Senior VP—Business &
Legal Affairs

MARYELLEN McLAUGHLIN
VP—Advertising & Custom
Publishing

GREGORY NOVECK
Senior VP—Creative Affairs

SUE POHJA
VP—Book Trade Sales

CHERYL RUBIN
Senior VP—
Brand Management

JEFF TROJAN
VP—Business Development:
DC Direct

BOB WAYNE
VP—Sales

JUMP, MAGAZINE, SUNDAY.

THESE THREE WORDS describe a big part of my childhood and my imagination. They are three manga magazines published weekly in Japan. Even after coming to America at the age of six, I read the imported magazines and they defined a good part of my adolescence. These magazines printed stories by everyone from great classical authors like Osamu Tezuka and Fujio Akatsuka, to contemporary masters like Naoki Urasawa, Akira Toriyama, and Rumiko Takahashi, just to name a few. The artists always brought stories and characters that reflected our current culture and times to the page. We grew with them and they grew with us.

Manga, like graphic novels or any piece of art, has many unique powers. It can unite us and inspire us. Through these art forms, we share a common bond, a passion that we could all lose ourselves in. It was always fascinating to me that every Tuesday when the weekly SHONEN JUMP came out, all the businessmen, in their suits and ties, would pick up a JUMP from a kiosk. They would ride the subways or buses, all silent, just immersing themselves in the world of manga. At that moment, these grown men were all experiencing the same thing. Manga is part of the Japanese culture and it defines a lot of who I am. At times it would be my romantic consultant, reading stories about a shy boy who is trying to muster the courage to ask a girl out. It would be my teacher as it pontificated on potential disruptions to the space/time continuum. It would be my hero as it continued to inspire me with journeys and tales of bravery and adventure. Sure, at lot of what I've "learned" isn't too applicable in real life, or would sometimes invite a slap in the face, but it enhanced my imagination and enriched our creativity.

We've all been affected by graphic novels in one form or another. As we grow, become adults, and gain responsibility, mangas are where I can find sanctuary and still be a kid. Imagination flows and it's a comfort to know that there are many, many others out there— from all walks of life—enjoying the same experience. If you're a kid, enjoy it. Savor it. Hold on to your imagination and your dreams. You can make a world a different place—but it begins with you. If you're an adult, enjoy. Relax. Let yourself be a kid again. Take a vacation and let your mind wander in the magical world of graphic novels. No one can stop us from learning. No one can stop us from dreaming. No one can stop us from believing.

Tim Kring created a beautiful world, laden with rich stories and deep characters. Many artists came together under his vision to create a fantastical piece of television called HEROES. What you see on television is a reflection of all the hard work put in by hundreds of people. But a mere television show couldn't contain us. There still are more stories to tell, that we *wanted* to tell but couldn't given the medium. Fortunately, we can share and expand through a different medium. We present you these graphic novels to help add another dimension to the HEROES universe. We hope you enjoy it and let yourself get lost in the HEROES world.

For Charlie,
Hiro Nakamura
(Masi Oka)

MADRAS, INDIA. 1982.

I USED TO BELIEVE THAT *MONSTERS* EXISTED. MY GRANDMOTHER TOLD ME STORIES...

...STORIES ABOUT THE GODDESS, *KALI*. HOW SHE IS *TEMPTED* TO KILL MANKIND. BUT, IF YOU ARE *DEVOTED*, KALI WILL ESCORT YOU INTO THE *AFTERLIFE*.

WHILE MY FAMILY WAS RELIGIOUS, MY FATHER WAS NOT. HE WAS A BRILLIANT GENETICIST. HE WOULD TELL ME...

THE WORLD IS AN AMAZING PLACE, MOHINDER, BUT THERE'S NO SUCH THING AS MONSTERS.

I CAME TO BELIEVE *EVERYTHING* MY FATHER SAID WAS TRUE.

CHUCK KIM *Story*
MARCUS TO *Art*
MARK ROSLAN *Digital inks*
DAVID MORAN *Colors*
COMICRAFT *Lettering*

BUT WHAT WAS I SUPPOSED TO *DO?*

WHEN I THINK ABOUT WHAT HE *DID* TO ME.

WHAT HE DID TO POOR *LORI TREMMEL.*

MMMRRRR...

I MEAN, WHO KNOWS HOW MANY *OTHER* GIRLS WENT THROUGH THAT?

HOW MANY OTHER GIRLS HE'D MOVE ON TO AFTER ME...

SOMETHING HAD TO BE *DONE.*

IS LIFE EVER
GOING TO BE
NORMAL AGAIN?

I REMEMBER TELLING MY *SON* ABOUT THE IMPORTANCE OF FOLLOWING *RULES*. GLAD HE CAN'T SEE ME *NOW*.

BUT I CAN'T *ROT AWAY* IN HERE, THINKING WHAT *COULD* HAVE BEEN. WATCHING MY OWN *BACK*.

SOMEONE NEEDS TO PROTECT *NIKI* AND *MICAH*. SOMEONE NEEDS TO FIND OUT WHO *FRAMED* ME.

SOMEONE NEEDS TO GET TO THE *BOTTOM* OF THIS.

57

-- though she was soon told that she did so in vain.

YOUR FATHER AIN'T *EVER* COMIN' BACK, SO YOU JUST PUT *THAT* OUT OF YOUR LITTLE OL' HEAD.

IF YOU'RE GONNA GO ON LIVIN' UNDER *THIS* ROOF, YOU'RE GONNA HAVE TO EARN YOUR *KEEP*.

And as immediately as her stepmother spoke, she was put to work.

EVERY DAY, RIGHT AFTER SCHOOL, YOU COME HOME AND GET RIGHT TO YOUR CHORES.

FIRST THING YOU DO IS VACUUM THE CARPETS.

Her life became an endless repetition of tasks carried out in silent servitude.

"Maybe if it's perfect," she thought. "Maybe then he'll come back..." And so she kept on.

As most adults know, life lived under the strict routine of work can pass you by in the blink of an eye --

All those years of suppressing her voice, keeping it deep down inside, made it so that when she finally spoke, no one could help but listen.

Her Stepmother's heart certainly listened, and stopped pumping the instant the command was uttered.

The Young Woman didn't know what power her voice held. She had changed in the course of an instant.

And nothing would be the same for her again.

Like her father had done those few years before, she left herself behind in that house now set ablaze.

"Move! You have to get out of here! Wake up!" she'd commanded.

But no matter what she said, she could not compel her Stepmother to move.

For what she ordered could not be undone.

And as she wiped away her tears, she wiped away her past.

ARE YOU *ALL RIGHT?* I'M GONNA CALL THE *POLICE.*

NO. JUST TAKE ME *AWAY* FROM HERE.

She had changed into someone else. Someone with a special gift.

WHERE DO YOU WANT TO *GO?*

WEST.

And to sever her new world of possibilities from the old, she decided to rename herself... *Eden.*

SALT LAKE CITY 125
LAS VEGAS 240

LIFE BEFORE EDEN

PIERLUIGI COTHRAN ✧ MARCUS TO
Story   *Art*
MARK ROSLAN ✧ PETER STEIGERWALD *Colors*
Digital inks   COMICRAFT *Lettering*

SUPER-HEROICS

IF I CAN GET HIM *HIGH* ENOUGH, HIS JETPACK WILL *FAIL*.

HARRISON WILCOX *Story* ✦ **MICAH GUNNELL** *Art*

PETER STEIGERWALD *Digital inks* ✦ **BETH SOTELO & DAVID MORAN** *Colors* **COMICRAFT** *Lettering*

THEN ALL I NEED IS TO HIT HIS SUIT HARD ENOUGH AGAINST SOMETHING TO *BREAK* IT.

LIKE THE *GROUND.*

THEN I MIGHT BE ABLE TO STOP HIM.

MOSSAD. ARMY INTELLIGENCE.

I ANALYZED. PLANNED *ATTACKS*. PLOTTED STRATEGIES. FOUND *WEAKNESSES*.

AT MY *BEST*, IT SEEMED AS IF I KNEW THE ENEMIES' MOVES BEFORE *THEY* DID.

THEY *PROMOTED* ME. AGAIN AND AGAIN. BUT I WAS STILL *MISERABLE*.

BUT I NEVER *GAVE UP*. I WAS DETERMINED TO SHOW THEM ALL EXACTLY WHAT I WAS *CAPABLE* OF.

AND THE TESTS WEREN'T ONLY *PHYSICAL.* THEY MEASURED MY BRAIN WAVES. THEY POKED AND PRODDED. THEY TOOK SAMPLES AND INJECTED WHAT THEY CALLED "VITAMINS".

HE SAID I WAS SPECIAL, BUT I FELT *USELESS.* WEEKS OF TESTING AND STILL *NOTHING.* MY MOTHER. MY GRANDMOTHER -- I *FAILED* THEM.

YOU *PROMISED* I WOULD SEE ACTION, BUT ALL I'VE SEEN IS *SNOW!*

WE'RE DOING THIS TO *HELP* YOU.

HELP ME? I DON'T EVEN KNOW WHAT YOU'RE TESTING ME FOR? OR *WHY?* I *WANT THE TRUTH!*

WHO'S *THOMPSON?*

HOW DO YOU KNOW THAT NAME?

HE JUST SENT YOU A TEXT MESSAGE. I JUST *READ* IT. WHAT DOES THAT MEAN, *MANIFEST?*

HANA, MY PHONE HASN'T *RUNG.*

BZZZZZZ

From: THOMPSON

When will she mainfest?

I ALWAYS HELD BACK. I NEVER TRUSTED ANYONE, LEAST OF ALL *MYSELF.* AND THEN, IT WAS AS IF I OPENED A *DOOR...*

93

WIRELESS

Part Two

ARON ELI COLEITE
& JOE POKASKI
Story

MICAH
GUNNELL
Art

MARK
ROSLAN
Digital inks

BETH SOTELO &
PETER STEIGERWALD
Colors

COMICRAFT
Lettering

...AND A *FLOOD* RUSHED IN. ALL THE E-MAILS, TEXT-MESSAGES AND SATELLITE TRANSMISSIONS FLOAT *INVISIBLY* AROUND THE WORLD.

I DONT KNOW HOW IT WAS POSSIBLE, BUT I COULD SEE, READ, SENSE EVERY *ONE* OF THEM. EVERY *FYI* MEMO. EVERY SAPPY "*I LOVE YOU*" TEXT. CANS AND CANS OF E-MAIL *SPAM*.

I KNEW ANY CODE CAN BE BROKEN. YOU JUST HAVE TO IDENTIFY THE *KEY.* I KNEW WITH ENOUGH EXPOSURE, WITH ENOUGH PRACTICE I WOULD *MASTER* THIS.

IT WAS BEAUTIFUL... BUT IT WAS *TOO MUCH.*

I WAS NEVER MEANT TO BE *ORDINARY*.

HEY, DAD -- YOU'RE GOOD WITH *NUMBERS* AND STUFF...

I DID EVERYTHING I *COULD* TO MAKE MYSELF STAND OUT. TRAINED *HARDER*. STUDIED MORE.

LEMME FINISH THIS *CALL* AND THEN YOU AND I WILL ATTACK YOUR HOMEWORK.

BUT, AS HARD AS I *TRIED* -- AS MUCH AS I *WANTED* IT -- THERE WERE ALWAYS *OBSTACLES* IN MY PATH.

THANKS, DAD.

ALL THAT *CHANGED* THE DAY I MET THE MAN WITH THE *HORN-RIMMED GLASSES*.

HANA, ARE YOU *IN POSITION*?

97

MY ABILITY IS MORE SUITED FOR THE *URBAN* JUNGLE THAN THIS ONE. GETTING PASSWORDS. STEALING DATA. *THAT* SORT OF THING.

BANG

OUT HERE, I ONLY HAVE *MYSELF* TO RELY ON.

ONES AND ZEROES AREN'T GOING TO GET ME OUT OF *THIS* MESS. BUT I ALREADY *KNEW* THAT.

HANA!

DAD? ARE YOU *COMING?*

I'LL BE RIGHT THERE.

THE MAN IN THE HORN-RIMMED GLASSES WANTED THE D.N.A ALTERATION FORMULA. HE CHANGED MY *LIFE.* SET ME *LOOSE* AGAINST THE BAD GUYS.

I OWE HIM *EVERYTHING.*

TANZANIA, AFRICA. NOW.

WELL, I REALLY *STEPPED IN IT.*

YOU'RE GONNA HATE ME FOR WHAT I DO NEXT. CALL ME ALL SORTS OF NAMES. *COWARD.* IDIOT. FOOL. BELIEVE ME... YOU DON'T HATE ME MORE THAN I HATE MYSELF.

I WAS IN MOSSAD LONG ENOUGH TO KNOW THAT *DIPLOMACY* IS THE ONLY WAY TO MAKE IT OUT OF HERE ALIVE.

LET THE POLITICIANS AND THE MAN WITH THE *HORN-RIMMED GLASSES* WORK OUT THE DETAILS.

I'M *C.I.A.*

DAR ES SALAAM, TANZANIA.

BUT, FOR ALL MY ABILITIES -- ALL MY TRAINING -- AND PLANNING...

WHAT?!?

...I DIDN'T SEE THIS ONE COMING.

THERE'S *NO RECORD* OF YOUR BEING IN THE C.I.A. NO SECRET BASE IN ALASKA. NO *SPECIAL OPERATIVES.*

HE *LIED* TO ME!

ALL THE NUMBERS YOU'VE *GIVEN* US HAVE BEEN DISCONNECTED.

IT'S *MY FAULT.* I WANTED TO BELIEVE HIM SO BADLY THAT I WALKED RIGHT INTO THE *LIE.* STUPID.

WHO ARE YOU *WORKING* FOR, MS. GITELMAN?

I REPLAY THE MOMENTS. LOOKING FOR AN *ANSWER.* WHERE DID I GO *WRONG?*

MISSOULA, MONTANA. NOW.

HAVE A GREAT DAY, SAMANTHA.

THANKS, DOROTHY.

I CAN SEE THE EMAILS *CLEARER* UP HERE. MAYBE IT'S THE FRESH AIR, MAYBE IT'S A *MENTAL* THING, BUT...

...IF SOMEONE WERE COMING AFTER ME -- I'D *KNOW.*

I SPEND MY TIME TRYING TO FIND INFORMATION ABOUT THE MAN WHO *DID* THIS TO ME. THE MAN WITH THE *HORN-RIMMED GLASSES.*

HE USED ME. MANIPULATED ME. *CHANGED* ME. I'M GOING TO FIND HIM. MAKE HIM *PAY.*

AND I'VE JUST LEARNED THAT I AM NOT *ALONE* IN THIS SENTIMENT.

NOW, I KNOW WHAT YOU'RE THINKING. THAT I HAVEN'T *CHANGED.* THAT I STILL HAVE *VENGEANCE* IN MY HEART.

I *LAID LOW.* NEW NAME. NEW *MISSION.* STAYED BELOW RADAR. NOT THAT I REALLY WORRIED ABOUT *THAT* MUCH ANYMORE.

BUT, THAT'S JUST *WHO I AM.*

SALT LAKE CITY
LAS VEGAS
SANTA FE

THREE WEEKS AGO.

MY NAME IS *THEODORE SPRAGUE*. I CAN EMIT 10,000 Ci OF RADIATION FROM MY BODY.

WAY *I* HEAR IT, YOU'RE HIDING SOME SERIOUS *PLUTONIUM*.

THEY'LL PROBABLY GIVE US *MEDALS* FOR TAKING DOWN A *TERRORIST*.

I'M NOT A TERRORIST. I HAVE NO IDEA *WHAT* I AM.

TWO YEARS AGO.

I USED TO BE HAPPY. I USED TO THINK I HAD *IT ALL*. A SOLID JOB. THE PERFECT WIFE. A *HAPPY FUTURE* LAID OUT FOR US.

BUT, IT'S NEVER THAT *EASY* IS IT?

ONE YEAR AGO.

IT ALL WENT AWAY. THIS ABILITY KILLED MY WIFE.

I WAS A NORMAL GUY. I DIDN'T *DESERVE* THIS.

AND NOW I'M GOING TO BE LOCKED AWAY. I'M NEVER GOING TO LEARN WHO *DID* THIS.

THE ANGER. IT *FESTERS*. AND THEN...

I ASKED HIM WHAT THE HYPO GUN WAS *FOR*. DID THEY USE IT TO *CHANGE* ME? TO MAKE ME INTO A *FREAK*? I WASN'T READY FOR HIS ANSWER.

THE HYPO GUN IS USED BY WILDLIFE RESEARCHERS. THEY *TRANQUILIZE* THEIR PREY, THEN USE THE HYPO GUN TO INJECT THE BEAST WITH A SPECIAL *ISOTOPE*.

THIS ISOTOPE CAN BE *REMOTELY DETECTED*. ALLOWING THE RESEARCHERS TO *TRACK* THE ANIMAL WHEREVER IT GOES.

WAS THAT WHAT I HAD *BECOME*? A *WILD ANIMAL* TO BE TRACKED AND STUDIED? GUESS I COULD *RUN* --

-- BUT I COULD NO LONGER *HIDE*.

To Be **CONTINUED...**

TWO DAYS AGO.

CAPTURED, TORTURED, THEN INJURED. IN *PODUNK,* TEXAS.

THESE BULLET HOLES WOULDN'T BE A *PROBLEM* IF I HAD JUST GOTTEN THAT *CHEERLEADER.*

HER DADDY WAS A DAMN GOOD *SHOT* FOR A GUY WHO NEEDS *CORRECTIVE LENSES.*

BUT NOT GOOD *ENOUGH.*

I CAN'T IMAGINE HE'S *NOT* COMING AFTER ME. AFTER WHAT I DID TO HIS *DAUGHTER.*

NOT TO MENTION HIS *WIFE.*

I NEED TO GET AS *FAR* AWAY FROM HERE AS POSSIBLE.

WHICH MEANS I NEED A *RIDE.*

ROAD KILL

NOBODY'S GOING TO EXPECT A *SURVIVOR*.

AND IF THEY *NEED* A BODY, MY FRIEND IN THE *TRAILER* WILL DO.

JOE POKASKI ◇ JASON BADOWER ◇ ANNETTE KWOK *Colors*
Story   *Art*   COMICRAFT *Lettering*

KRISTY. IT'S *KRISTY*, RIGHT?

HE TOLD ME I WAS GOING TO BE A *MOVIE STAR*. I WASN'T DOING ANYTHING WRONG.

OF *COURSE* YOU WEREN'T. JUST GO BACK TO YOUR *PARENTS*. OKAY? RUN. *FAST*.

HEY, WHATEVER YOU THINK I'M *DOING*, I'M *NOT*, OKAY? I *SWEAR*. I...

YOU *SICK* SON OF A --

SLAM

HOW MANY PEOPLE ARE HOOKED INTO THIS *FEED*? HOW MANY PEOPLE *PAID* YOU TO WATCH THAT LITTLE GIRL TAKE OFF HER *CLOTHES*?

IT'S NOT...

I WILL *SHOOT* YOU. I WILL PUT A BULLET IN YOUR *BRAIN*. NOW TELL ME. *HOW MANY?*

THREE HUNDRED AND FIFTY-TWO.

IT'S A SICK, SAD *WORLD*. WE TRY NOT TO *THINK* ABOUT IT, BUT WHEN THE REALITY IS STARING YOU IN THE FACE, YOU MUST *ACT*.

140

THE ONLY PERSON I TRUSTED TO *HELP* ME WAS A WOMAN I HAD *TRAINED*.

HANA GITELMAN HAD THE MOST EXTRAORDINARY *ABILITY* -- TO SEE AND HEAR EVERY BIT OF DATA ON THE INTERNET, SWIRLING AROUND HER LIKE LEAVES IN THE WIND. I CALLED HER *WIRELESS*.

THEY WERE *CLOSING IN*. I HAD TO GET AN *E-MAIL* OUT.

AND *HOPE*.

AND PRAY THAT SHE WAS *OUT* THERE.

LISTENING.

COME ON... *ANSWER* ME! *ANSWER!*

MAYBE HANA HASN'T *FORGIVEN* ME FOR TRICKING HER INTO WORKING FOR THE *BAD GUYS,* AND LEAVING HER FOR *DEAD* IN THE MIDDLE OF THE SERENGETI.

ROUTE 66.
110 M.P.H.

Parkman and Spray, and he. I know you helped them. I'm changing side, Hana. I need your help to shut it all down

WIRELESS Instant message

Conversation View Edit Actions Help

Wireless

Wireless: I'll do it.

WHOEVER'S FOLLOWING ME WILL JUST THINK I WENT FOR A *LATTE.*

AND NOW THAT I'VE GOT *WIRELESS* WORKING WITH ME ON THE OUTSIDE, MY PLAN TO BRING DOWN THE PEOPLE I WORK FOR, AND PROTECT MY *DAUGHTER,* JUST MIGHT *WORK.*

AS LONG AS MY PARTNER CAN *SHOOT* STRAIGHT...

WHAT DID YOU *EXPECT?* THAT I'D BREAK INTO THE PENTAGON *GUNS A' BLAZING?*

I NEED TO ACCOMPLISH THIS *MISSION.*

I NEED *ANSWERS* TO MY QUESTIONS.

LOOKS LIKE I'M OFF TO A *GOOD START.*

To Be Continued...

Date: November 15, 1968; Location: Mekong River Delta, Vietnam.

We were forty miles into enemy territory, on a mission to recover a downed A4 Skyhawk.

Politicians were in Paris trying to broker peace. Bombing was supposed to stop a week before.

So according to the U.S. Military, the Skyhawk was never even there. We had to make sure that squared with reality.

To ensure plausible deniability, we didn't even know each others' identities. No dog tags, no rank insignia, no personal effects.

To save the politicians' good names, we gave up ours.

We went by names given to us by Uncle Sam, but that didn't change who we were...

Mine's DALLAS.

LAREDO. Demolitions expert. Was plowing his Dad's farm by age 13.

SAN ANTONIO. Communications. Heavyweight Gold Gloves Champ of Kansas City, MO.

AMARILLO. Gunboat pilot. Had a girl named Marcy back home.

AUSTIN. Medic. Always had his nose buried in a book.

Time spent under the constant threat of death... it brings men together in a way that tosses formalities aside.

Even so, seven days is a long time to go without hearing your name. Distractions only go so far...

THIS TABLE *EVEN*? EVERYTHING KEEPS SLIDING MY WAY.

HELL, DALLAS. I'M *OUT*.

And tensions ran high.

WHATCHA *GOT* THERE?

Something as simple as a book can make a soldier feel as if home is never too far away.

PERSONAL CONTRABAND? THIS IS ENOUGH TO GET YOU *COURT-MARTIALED*.

ALTHOUGH, BEIN' 40 MILES INTO *ENEMY TERRITORY*, YOU'D JUST AS SOON GET THROWN *OVERBOARD*.

But it could also blow our mission.

GOT SOMETHIN' TO *SAY* FOR YOURSELF, SOLDIER?

WHAT'D YOU *DO* TO ME?!

But at the time, it scared the living hell out of me.

It scared me more than Charlie shooting bullets at me every day for the last two years...

TELL ME WHAT YOU *DID*...

...because at least Charlie was something I could understand.

I COULDN'T LET YOU LOSE YOURSELF OUT HERE.

WAR BUDDIES
Part 2 of Six
UNKNOWN SOLDIERS

ANDREW CHAMBLISS & PIERLUIGI COTHRAN
Story

ADAM ARCHER
Pencils

MARK ROSLAN
Digital Inks

BETH SOTELO
Colors

COMICRAFT
Lettering

Day five. Three men down. And I didn't even know their names.

Just aliases. I'm Dallas. Austin, the other survivor, is the medic. 16 kills, still looking for our downed pilots.

AGAIN, WHERE'S THE PLANE?

I DON'T -- ACK!

Patience, along with supplies, was dwindling. We needed answers. Fast.

I wasn't comfortable with Austin. The way he questioned me.

HEAL HIM.

HOW MANY TIMES ARE YOU GONNA DO THIS, DALLAS? IT'S JUST SICK.

The way he could fix people when they should be getting last rites. It wasn't natural.

But it was useful.

JUST DO IT.

Austin applied first aid to the informant as I continued the debriefing.

NOW TELL ME EVERYTHING YOU KNOW...

...OR I BREAK YOUR JAW FOR THE TENTH TIME.

Four hours later, he gave us what we needed.

We reached the plane the next morning. There were no survivors.

We were too late. Our rescue was a failure.

WAR BUDDIES Part 3 of Six

DJ DOYLE
Story

ADAM ARCHER
Pencils

MARK ROSLAN
Digital Inks

BETH SOTELO
Colors

COMICRAFT
Lettering

NO MORE BULLETS LEFT. HE PUT UP A *FIGHT* AT LEAST.

BRING THEM *BACK.*

YOU KNOW I *CAN'T.* I CAN ONLY HEAL THE *LIVING.*

FREAK.

FREAK? YOU COULDN'T *HANDLE* THE *PAIN* THIS HAS BROUGHT ME.

What happened at the river and plane would not go unavenged. With C4 explosives from the plane and 7 clips of ammunition between us: the village of Au Co was gonna be toast.

WE HEAD IN ON MY MARK. START WITH THE HUT ON THE FAR LEFT, I'LL START AT THE RIGHT. MEET IN THE MIDDLE.

LOOKS LIKE A LOT OF CIVILIANS.

This was our new mission. With "Austin," a man whose real name I didn't even know. To end the war.

But to him, I was "Dallas." Government code name for government code name. I guess that made it fair.

YEAH? AND WHAT KIND OF CIVILIAN CARRIES A M-16?

"IT DOESN'T ADD UP. THEY'D NEED ALL KINDS OF EQUIPMENT TO FARM THIS MUCH LAND."

The truth was -- the entire valley was created by ████████████████████

We had enough explosives to blow up half the village, get them running -- the fires would take care of the rest.

RIG THE NEXT THREE AND STAND BY. AT 15:30 LIGHT THIS PLACE UP. I'LL BE DIRECTLY ACROSS.

COPY THAT.

The village was heavily armed.

THWACK

We had to be perfect. We had to be brutal.

FOUR...

THREE...

TWO...

ONE...

15:29:57

15:29:58

15:29:59

WAR BUDDIES

Part 4 of Six

TIMM KEPPLER — Story
JASON BADOWER — Pencils
ANNETTE KWOK — Digital Inks & Colors
COMICRAFT — Lettering

Scorched earth.

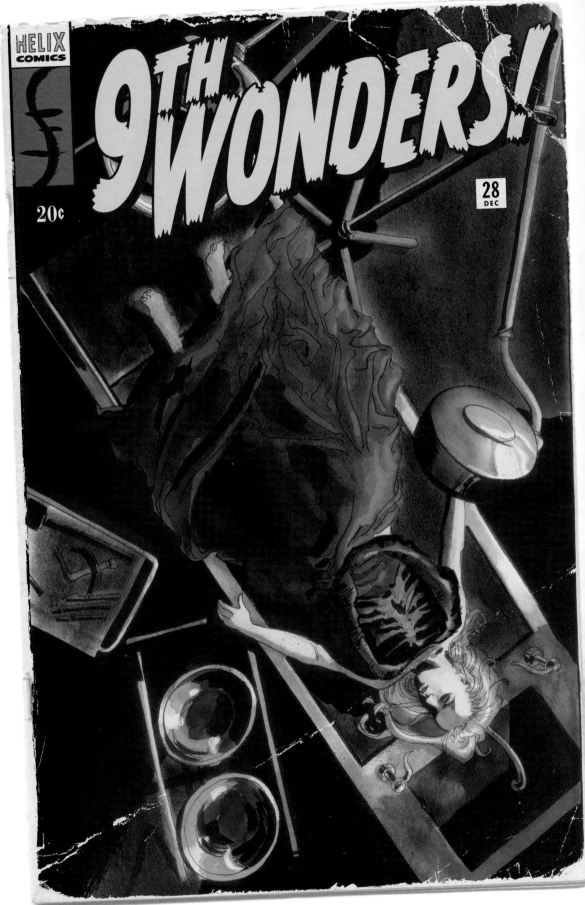

A secret mission to find one of
our downed jets turned into taking
out an entire enemy village. We all
thought Au Co was the name of the
village. It wasn't. It was a girl.
I had to kill her.

Au Co, ▓▓▓▓▓▓▓ with
just a wave of her arms.

HARRISON WILCOX
& OLIVER GRIGSBY ◇ JASON
BADOWER
Story *Pencils*

ANNETTE KWOK ◇ COMICRAFT
Digital Inks & Colors *Lettering*

Days earlier, most of the unit was gunned down. Only Austin the medic and I were left. I was shot in the chest.

I should have died.

Austin ████████ ██████ No scars, no blood. Nothing. I should be dead.

He didn't want to go through with the mission. To kill Au Co. Understandable. ████████████████ she was special.

But Austin couldn't see the bigger picture.

Au Co had to die. I wouldn't let him save her. Not like he saved me.

YOU'LL THANK ME FOR THIS ONE DAY. WE JUST SAVED A LOT OF LIVES.

Austin's refusal to admit the truth ended up costing me greatly.

Silenced. Discharged. Ignored. The desire to ████████████████ ████████████████ destroyed everything I had built for myself in the military.

My life, my family, for what it was, had become...pointless.

DING DONG

Until Austin showed up at my home. Older and different. With what appeared to be a change of heart.

I OWE YOU AN APOLOGY.

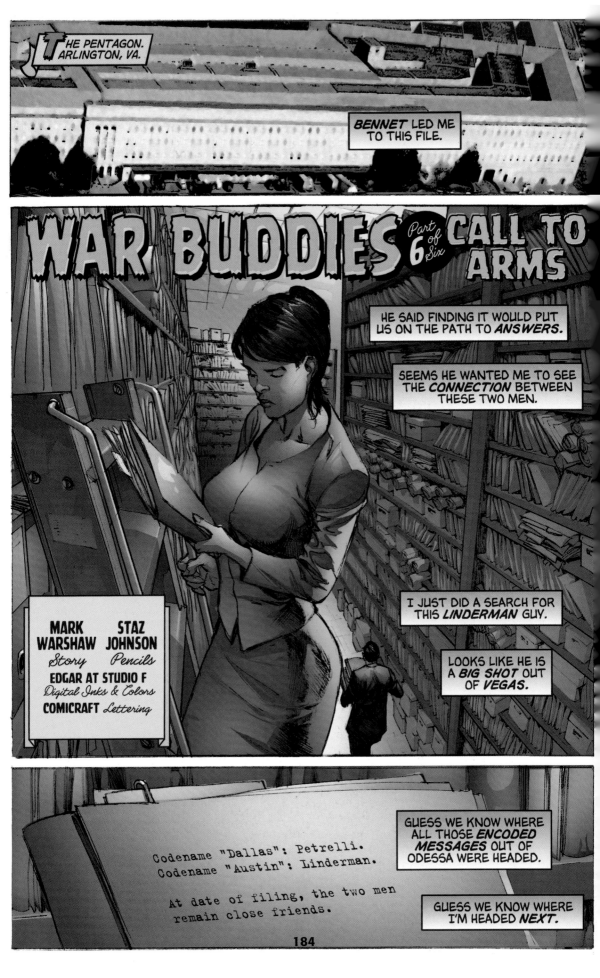

BENNET LED ME TO THIS FILE.

WAR BUDDIES'
Part 6 of Six
CALL TO ARMS

HE SAID FINDING IT WOULD PUT US ON THE PATH TO ANSWERS.

SEEMS HE WANTED ME TO SEE THE CONNECTION BETWEEN THESE TWO MEN.

I JUST DID A SEARCH FOR THIS LINDERMAN GUY.

LOOKS LIKE HE IS A BIG SHOT OUT OF VEGAS.

MARK WARSHAW
Story

STAZ JOHNSON
Pencils

EDGAR AT STUDIO F
Digital Inks & Colors

COMICRAFT Lettering

Codename "Dallas": Petrelli.
Codename "Austin": Linderman.

At date of filing, the two men remain close friends.

GUESS WE KNOW WHERE ALL THOSE ENCODED MESSAGES OUT OF ODESSA WERE HEADED.

GUESS WE KNOW WHERE I'M HEADED NEXT.

CASEY SMITH'S APARTMENT.

I'VE GOT WHAT I *NEED*.

HAD MORE TIME THAN I *EXPECTED* HERE.

SAMANTHA?

MY NEW FRIEND CASEY MUST BE A *DEEP* SLEEPER.

I NEED TO REPORT A POSSIBLE *HIGH LEVEL* SECURITY BREACH, SIR!

IF THIS LINDERMAN GUY WANTS PETRELLI TO WIN SO BAD, IT *CAN'T* BE A GOOD THING.

TO UNRIG AN ELECTION IS A *TALL ORDER.*

I'M GOING TO NEED A LITTLE HELP FROM MY *FRIENDS.*

WANT TO HELP HANA RUIN LINDERMAN'S PLANS? FOLLOW THE DIRECTIONS IN THE TEXT MESSAGE OR E-MAIL TITLED *"CALL TO ARMS"* FOR NEXT STEPS.

IF YOU ARE NOT A REGISTERED *HEROES 360* USER, GO HERE: www.samantha48616e61.com TO JOIN THE CAUSE NOW!

AFTER FIVE YEARS OF MANIPULATING TIME, I BEGAN TO *UNDERSTAND* IT.

TIME WAS NOT A LINE OR A FABRIC, BUT THE PRODUCT OF LIVES, INTERWEAVED.

SYLAR'S LIFELINE WAS CRUCIAL, OF COURSE. HE WAS THE *BOMB*.

I STABBED HIM BEFORE HE EXPLODED, BUT HE *REGENERATED*.

HE WAS ABLE TO DO THIS BECAUSE HE KILLED *CLAIRE BENNET*, THE CHEERLEADER.

SO TO SAVE THE WORLD, I NEEDED TO FIND SOMEONE FROM *THAT* TIME TO SAVE THE CHEERLEADER.

SOMEONE I KNEW WOULD *NOT FAIL*.

PETER PETRELLI.

AT LEAST IN THERE, NO ONE WAS TRYING TO *KILL* ME.

AT LEAST I KNEW WHO I WAS -- *PRISONER NIKI.*

I'VE BEEN A LOT OF THINGS.

LIVED A LOT OF LIVES.

PICKED UP A FEW TRICKS FROM *EACH* OF THEM, I SUPPOSE.

BUT *NEVER,* IN A MILLION YEARS, WOULD I HAVE GUESSED, THAT OF *ALL THINGS...*

...IT WOULD BE THE *POLE-DANCING* THAT WOULD SAVE MY HIDE.

WALLS Part 2

JOE POKASKI
Story

MICHAEL GAYDOS
Art

EDGAR AT STUDIO F *Colors*
COMICRAFT *Lettering*

AND JUST LIKE *THAT,* WE LEFT.

WE WERE *FREE.*

SORT OF.

WHEN CAN I TALK TO MY *WIFE?*

YOU ARE ALL STILL IN *DANGER.*

WE'RE GOING TO ARRANGE TRANSPORTATION TO A SPECIAL FACILITY IN TEXAS...

WHAT'S IN *TEXAS?*

MOST OF MY FELLOW INMATES HAD FAMILIES TO REUNITE WITH. *LIVES* TO RESUME.

I HAD *NO IDEA* WHAT TO DO NEXT.

YOU WERE *GREAT* BACK THERE, BY THE WAY.

THANKS.

I'VE LIVED A LOT OF LIVES.

LET ME KNOW IF YOU NEED ANY *HELP* WITH ANYTHING... LIKE TRACKING DOWN YOUR *FAMILY.*

THAT'S NOT NECESSARY. I DON'T REALLY *HAVE* A FAMILY ANYMORE.

OH.

BUT THEY ALL *ENDED* THE DAY THE *BOMB* WENT OFF.

WHO WOULD I BECOME *NOW?*

WHEN I WAS A LITTLE GIRL, I IMAGINED HEAVEN WAS FILLED WITH CLOUDS AND ANGELS WITH BEAUTIFUL FEATHERED WINGS.

THE HEAVENS ARE FILLED WITH MECHANICAL ANGELS -- *SATELLITES.* THOUSANDS AND THOUSANDS OF SATELLITES.

AND LIKE ANGELS -- THEY WATCH OVER US. THEY SEE EVERYTHING WE DO. EVERY CALL WE MAKE. EVERY E-MAIL WE WRITE. THEY KNOW HOW WE LIVE.

SEARCHING... TARGET: HANA GITELMAN...

AND THEY KNOW HOW WE *DIE.*

THIS *ISN'T* HOW I EXPECTED TO DIE.

THE *DEATH* OF HANA GITELMAN

ARON ELI COLEITE
Story

JASON BADOWER
Art & Color

COMICRAFT
Lettering

Part 1

ACCORDING TO NEWS REPORTS THAT DAY, MANY CELL PHONES AND E-MAIL PROVIDERS SAID THE TEMPORARY *GLITCH* IN SERVICE WAS DUE TO *MAGNETIC ACTIVITY.*

I KNEW IT WAS BECAUSE OF *ME.*

I'M GLAD TO SEE MY *RIDE* HASN'T LEFT *WITHOUT* ME.

EVEN IN MY WILDEST DREAMS, I *NEVER* EXPECTED TO BE DOING *THIS...*

THIS IS HOW THE *ANGELS* SEE THE EARTH -- OBSERVING -- WATCHING -- *EVERYTHING.*

AND FOR A MOMENT I *FORGET* ABOUT THE MISSION. AND I FORGET ABOUT THE *MANIPULATIONS.* AND THE PAIN. AND THE *DEATH.*

I *HAD* TO DO IT. IT WAS THE ONLY *CHOICE.* IT WAS THE ONLY WAY THAT PEOPLE LIKE ME COULD BE *SAFE.*

AND I DIDN'T *WANT* TO BE A MARTYR. AND I WASN'T DOING IT FOR *REVENGE,* OR BECAUSE I HAD A *DEATH WISH.* I DID IT BECAUSE IT WAS THE *RIGHT THING* TO *DO.*

SO, I SUPPOSE IN A LOT OF WAYS -- IT'S *EXACTLY* HOW I EXPECTED TO DIE.

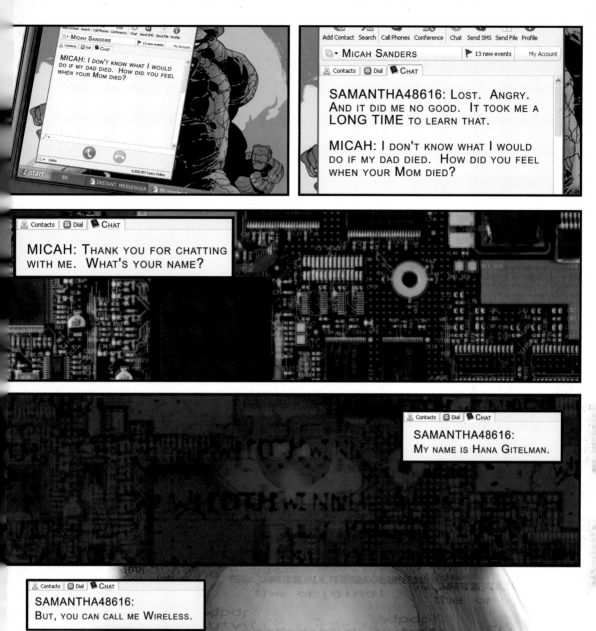

MICAH: I DON'T KNOW WHAT I WOULD DO IF MY DAD DIED. HOW DID YOU FEEL WHEN YOUR MOM DIED?

Add Contact   Search   Call Phones   Conference   Chat   Send SMS   Send File   Profile

MICAH SANDERS   13 new events   My Account

Contacts   Dial   CHAT

SAMANTHA48616: LOST. ANGRY. AND IT DID ME NO GOOD. IT TOOK ME A LONG TIME TO LEARN THAT.

MICAH: I DON'T KNOW WHAT I WOULD DO IF MY DAD DIED. HOW DID YOU FEEL WHEN YOUR MOM DIED?

Contacts   Dial   CHAT

MICAH: THANK YOU FOR CHATTING WITH ME. WHAT'S YOUR NAME?

Contacts   Dial   CHAT

SAMANTHA48616: MY NAME IS HANA GITELMAN.

Contacts   Dial   CHAT

SAMANTHA48616: BUT, YOU CAN CALL ME WIRELESS.

Contacts   Dial   CHAT

SAMANTHA48616: AND THE TRUTH IS, DEATH IS NEVER QUITE WHAT YOU EXPECT IT TO BE. IT MIGHT SEEM LIKE AN ENDING, BUT REALLY...

SAMANTHA48616:
...THE JOURNEY IS JUST BEGINNING.

THE HEROES INTERVIEW

EXECUTIVE PRODUCER **JEPH LOEB** TALKS WITH SERIES WRITERS **ARON ELI COLEITE** AND **JOE POKASKI**

JEPH: A comic book version of HEROES seems like a no-brainer, but how did it come about?

ARON & JOE: If Tim Kring was the general who ordered a strike on the American zeitgeist with this crazy show called "Heroes"—I guess you could consider us to be some of the first boots on the ground. Before the Pilot was even picked up, we talked extensively with Tim about the online component of the show. How to extend the storytelling from one hour on a Monday into an immersive fan experience.

The online comic was one of the first ideas that came to mind. We had so many stories to tell and there was only so much room in the TV show—so we decided that we could tell these alternate stories in the comics. The stories could be deeper, broader and reveal more secrets about our characters. It was also a way to tell stories that would be otherwise unproduceable on our show.

But this is different from traditional comics, right? It's online and only 5 or 6 pages a shot.

The goal was to put out 22 pages a month, like most comics, but to come out weekly like

a television show. So the math dictated 5 or 6 pages per installment and we lucked into the perfect length for a Heroes Webcomic.

Like the scenes or stories in the pilot or in subsequent episodes—the webcomic would be what we called "Haiku," short but purposeful. Every panel meaning something.

It actually forced us to be better, more concise storytellers—we weren't allowed to ramble or wander. We had to tell unique, exciting and fulfilling stories in 5 pages.

You've filled in some of the gaps in the stories from the show. Do you feel like people who watch the show have to read these to know what's going on?

Not at all. In fact, our first rule going in was that you didn't have to read the comic to enjoy the show, but it created an enhanced experience if you did.

On the other side, we wanted people who did watch the show and read the comic to feel rewarded—that they were taking part of something larger and give them real emotional and important stories—not just fluff or filler.

Michael Turner, Phil Jimenez, Aspen, Nanci Quesada, Alex Ross, and Jim Lee—and those are just for starters. How did the comic book community get involved with what could otherwise be seen as just another licensed property?

For starters, we had a big gun—this guy named Jeph Loeb. It's not a stretch to call him a living legend. And on top of that, a ridiculously large amount of people in the industry who love him—and would jump in front of a train for him. We're not sure if it was that, or his ability to sell a good idea, but soon we had an amazing bullpen of writers and artists working for us.

The short format had a little to do with it too. Many comic book artists pour their hearts and soul onto each page. At 22 pages per comic that is a lot of soul pouring. It's easier to get a top-notch artist for 5 or 6 pages. It's like keeping a friend out at a bar by saying "one more drink." Who doesn't want one more?

Are there new writers we can look forward to next season?

We've already got a bunch of great writers from the show. We've also been joined by veterans like Steven Seagle, Joe Kelly and Duncan Rouleau. But, we've also been fortunate to get some young comic book scribes to join our crew like Mark Sable and Christine Boylen.

On top of that, we've got an amazing staff of up and coming brilliant minds that help us with the impossible task of writing one of these a week. Writers like Harry Wilcox, Oliver Grigsby, Chris Zatta, Jim Martin, Pierluigi Cothran, Timm Keppler and Andrew Chambliss. Watch out for these names—you will see them in the future.

And rumor has it that a certain writer whose name rhymes with SCHMEPH SCHMOEB will introduce a new character called "Rachel Red, Robogirl."

You had to start even before anyone had seen the show. What was that like?

In a lot of ways, it was liberating. As with the show, all we could do is tell the most exciting stories that you would want to experience yourself. Just go for it, because there was no audience reaction to be reactionary towards.

But of course, in the back of your head, for the show and the webcomic, there's the whole "what if you threw a Television Show and nobody arrives" concern eating at the back of your head.

Are there some stories you CAN'T or WON'T tell as comics?

We don't want to touch anything that should be seen on the television. For example, we were tempted to tell the webcomic of how H.R.G. got assigned to be Claire's father— but we knew that would be better served on the show—as everyone finally saw in "Company Man."

There's a new online story up every week! How do you do that when some monthly comics ⁚koff-*Ultimates*-koff⁚ sometimes can't make shipping!

Most of that lies with a guy named Mark Warshaw. And Chuck Kim. They keep the trains running on time. Sometimes we run right up to the wire and deliver the pages moments before they need to go live, but even so—we have yet to miss a deadline.

Fortunately we're able to line up the stories with the episodes so we can try to keep ahead of the curve and have scripts generated quickly and early.

If you could have a crossover with any of the DC characters, what would your dream team-up be?

I think everyone would want to see the Supergirl/Claire team up. A Peter/Superman throwdown might be fun as well. And of course Green Lantern/Ando would be a classic matchup.

So...are you comic book writers or graphic novelists? Remember, this is how you'll be defined for the rest of your lives...

Is there a third choice?

You're both pretty big comic geeks. What's it like now, creating your own universe? What do you read? Do you buy comics on a weekly basis?

Each Wednesday (ideally) we actually make our trek to the local store. A big shout-out to our friends at Meltdown who take good care of us every week. We read a lot of everything. Bendis. Millar. Johns. And of course everything that Loeb puts out. It's one of the rare pleasures in life to go to a comic book store with Jeph Loeb and see the fans pointing and whispering.

Are there stories that you can tell only in this graphic novel form?

There are certainly ones that are easier— because there are no production restraints. For example, when Hana Gitelman went to China to stow away on the Space Shuttle so she could spacewalk to a satellite and ride it down into the burning atmosphere. That would have been difficult to produce.

Fire. Space. Polar Ice Caps. Jungles of Africa. Battles with Indian gods and confrontations with Australian rock formations. There is no limit in this format. It's very rewarding.